MY COOL, AWESOME, INCREDIBLE, FUN, RAD DAD

AN ILLUSTRATED TRIBUTE TO ALL THE DADS OUT THERE

DOG 'n' BONE

RUS HUDDA

Published in 2018 by Dog 'n' Bone Books
An imprint of Ryland Peters & Small Ltd
20–21 Jockey's Fields   341 E 116th St
London WC1R 4BW   New York, NY 10029

www.rylandpeters.com

10 9 8 7 6 5 4 3 2 1

A CIP catalog record for this book is available from
the Library of Congress and the British Library.

ISBN: 978 1 911026 51 8

Printed in China

Cover design: Geoff Borin
Illustrator: Rus Hudda

CONTENTS

My Dad's the...

My Dad's the rockingest...

He plays the loudest guitar.

He can beat any video game.

MY DAD'S THE GREATEST...

He pushes me the highest on the swings.

MY DAD'S THE FUNNEST...

He loves to play with me
in the pool.

MY DAD'S THE ARTSIEST...

He draws the most
excellent cartoons.

My Dad's the most adventurous...

He takes me on
epic bike rides.

My Dad's the prettiest...

He loves a bit of pampering.

MY DAD'S THE SPEEDIEST...

He drives his car
the fastest.

MY DAD'S THE SLICKEST...

He's got all the latest styles.

My Dad's
the yummiest...

He bakes
the tastiest cakes.

MY DAD'S THE MOST PRACTICAL...

He builds the most ginormous sandcastles.

My Dad's the greatest...

He makes every day exciting.

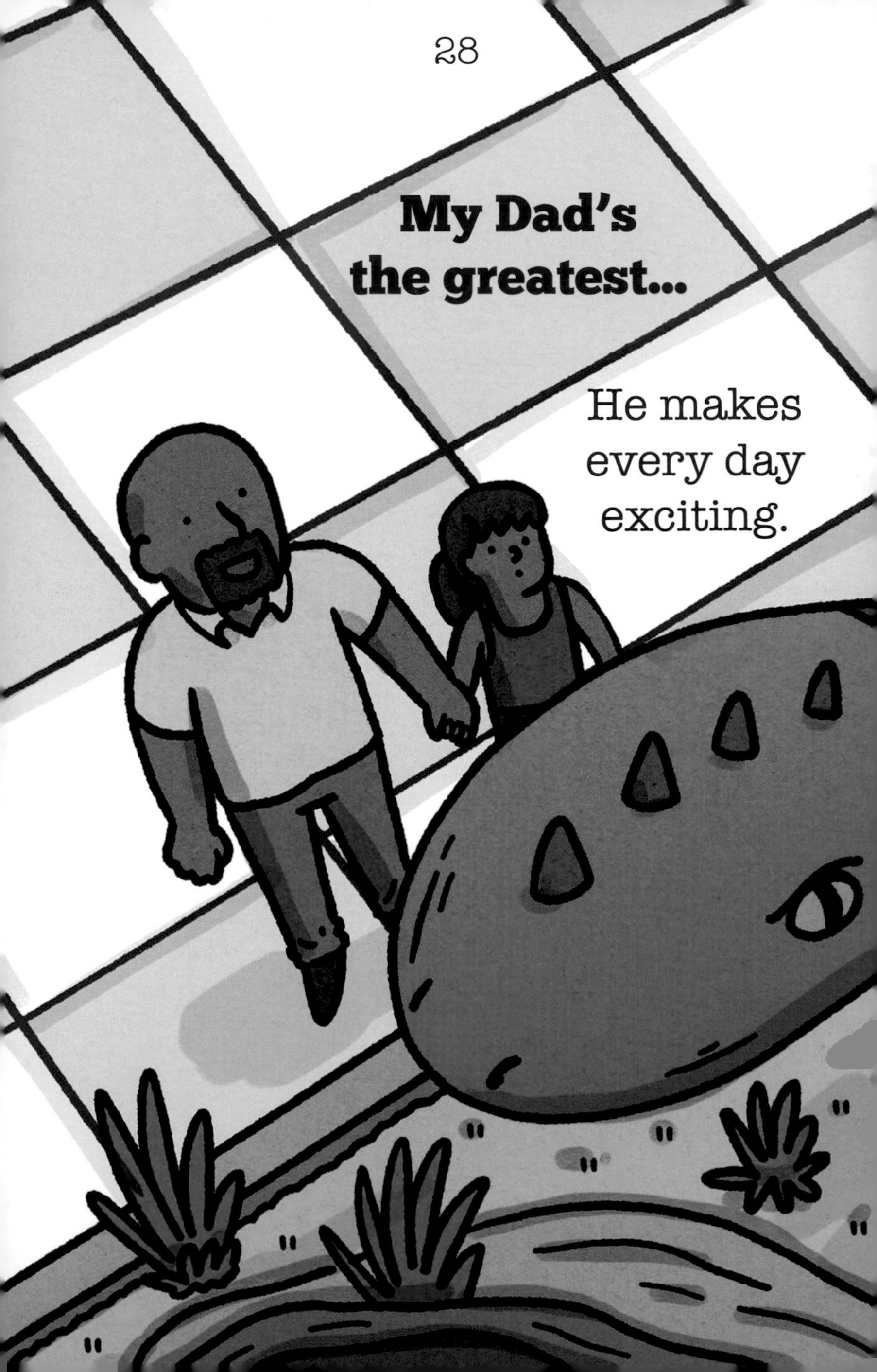

MY DAD'S
THE SPOOKIEST...

He tells the creepiest
ghost stories.

MY DAD'S THE MOST INSPIRATIONAL...

The books he reads to me take us on the most incredible journeys.

MY DAD'S THE CHEFIEST...

He cooks the finger-lickingest breakfasts.

MY DAD'S THE MOST INVENTIVE...

He creates
the best forts.

MY DAD'S THE WILDEST...

He takes me camping
in the great outdoors.

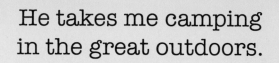

He makes the biggest splashes.

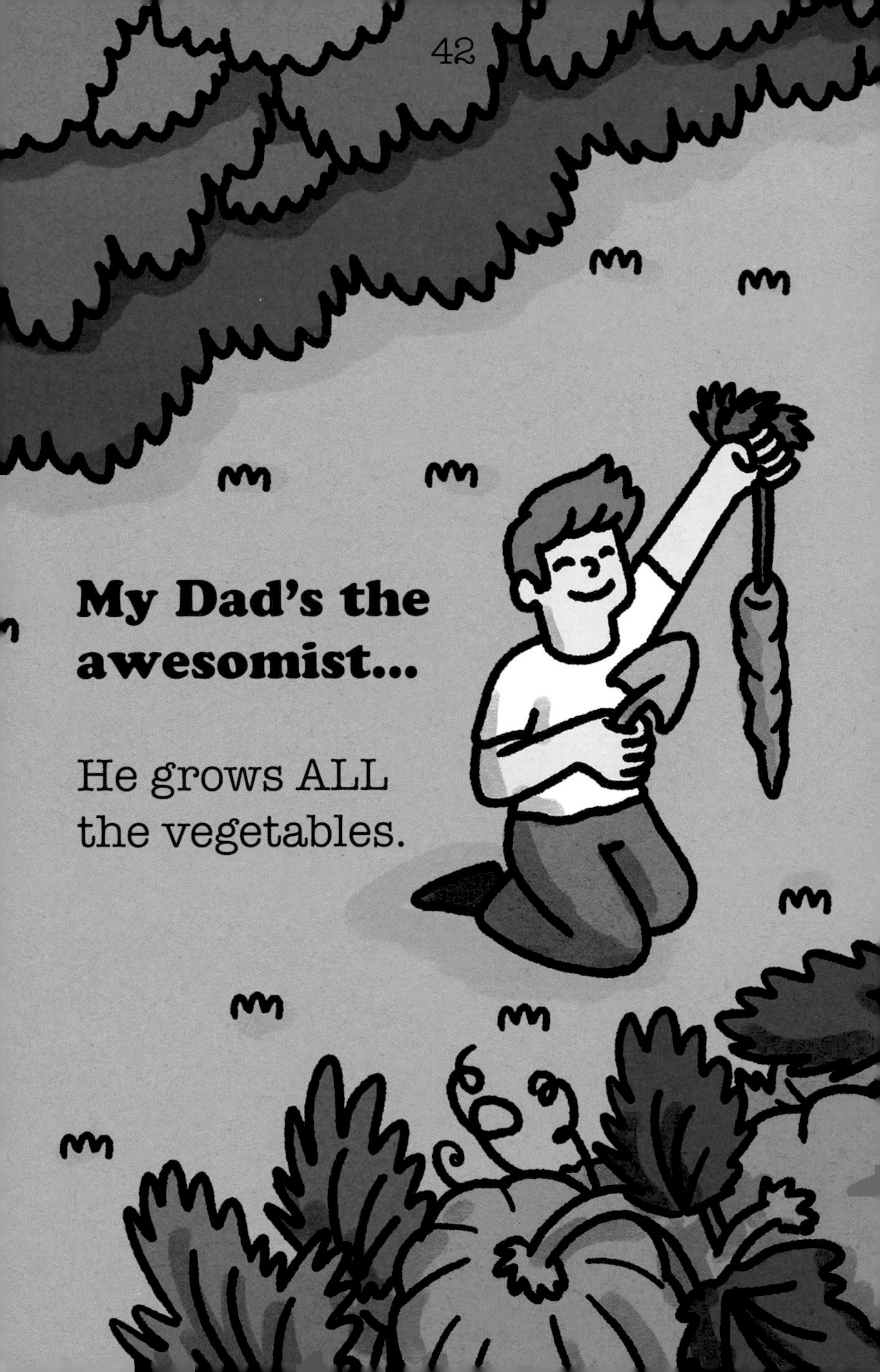

My Dad's the awesomist...

He grows ALL the vegetables.

He sings my favorite
songs in the mirror.

MY DAD'S THE MOST FANTASTIC...

He helps me to learn more
about my hobbies.

He knows everything about anything.

My Dad's the messiest...

He paints the prettiest pictures.

My Dad's the Wackiest...

He does the
silliest impressions.

My Dad's the tallest...

_____

_____

He carries me the highest
on his shoulders.

My Dad's the happiest...

He's got the most amazing movie collection.

My Dad's the bravest...

He's not scared
of anything.

MY DAD'S THE FUNKIEST...

He owns all the best party-starting records.

MY DAD'S THE BEST...

And there's no Dad better.

ACKNOWLEDGMENTS

My Dad is so cool because he taught me not to worry so much.

My Mum is so cool because she always supported me.

My wife is so cool because she's strong minded.

My daughter is so cool because she always makes me proud.

My cat is so cool because she welcomes me home.

Pete Jorgensen and Dog 'n' Bone Books are so cool because they have great taste in books.